# FOUND:
## GOD'S PEACE

# FOUND:
## GOD'S PEACE

EXPERIENCE TRUE
FREEDOM FROM ANXIETY
IN EVERY CIRCUMSTANCE

# JOHN MACARTHUR

DAVID C COOK

*transforming lives together*

FOUND: GOD'S PEACE
Published by David C Cook
4050 Lee Vance Drive
Colorado Springs, CO 80918 U.S.A.

Integrity Music Limited, a Division of David C Cook
Brighton, East Sussex BN1 2RE, England

The graphic circle C logo is a registered trademark of David C Cook.

Unless otherwise noted, Scripture quotations are taken from the
New American Standard Bible®, Copyright © 1960, 1995 by The
Lockman Foundation. Used by permission. (www.Lockman.org.)
Scripture quotations marked KJV are taken from the King James
Version of the Bible. (Public Domain); NIV are taken from the
Holy Bible, New International Version®, NIV®. Copyright ©
1973, 1984 by Biblica, Inc.™ Used by permission of Zondervan.
All rights reserved worldwide. www.zondervan.com; and TLB
are taken from The Living Bible, © 1971, Tyndale House
Publishers, Wheaton, IL 60189. Used by permission. The author
has added italics to Scripture quotations for emphasis.

Library of Congress Control Number 2014948631
ISBN 978-0-7814-1276-6
eISBN 978-1-4347-0894-6

© 1993, 2015 John MacArthur
Published in association with the literary agency
of Wolgemuth & Associates, Inc.
The content of this book is derived from Anxious for Nothing
© 1993, 2012 John MacArthur, ISBN 978-1-4347-0297-5.

The Team: Ingrid Beck, Amy Konyndyk, Jack
Campbell, Helen Macdonald, Karen Athen
Cover Design: Nick Lee
Cover Photo: Shutterstock

Printed in the United States of America
First Edition 2015

6 7 8 9 10 11 12 13 14 15

032520

# CONTENTS

# INTRODUCTION

*Anxiety*, *fear*, *worry*, and *stress* are familiar words in our day and familiar experiences to many. Extreme displays of anxiety are often related to an unfounded fear so overwhelming and so overpowering that it clutches a person's heart, forces the heart to beat faster, produces chills or perspiration, and makes the person feel completely unable to cope with the moment.

One woman wrote grippingly of her experience with panic attacks. She began, "While interviewing with my prospective employer, something terrifying happened. The windowless room where the interview took place closed in around me, the air became thin.

My throat tightened and the rushing in my head
became deafening. All I could think was, *I've got to
get out.* My mind and heart raced for what seemed an
eternity as I feigned composure. Somehow, I made it
through the meeting without giving my interviewer a
clue I had been seconds away from fleeing his office
or passing out on the spot.... I endured a rush of
the fight-or-flight instinct one usually experiences in
life-threatening situations."[1] The reality, however, was
that she wasn't in a life-threatening situation.

Anxiety is, at its core, an inappropriate response
in light of circumstances; it's very different from
the cares and concerns in life that cause people to
attend to business in a responsible way. Stress and
pressure, instead of being things to avoid, strengthen
us to accomplish the challenges God sets before us
in life. The apostle Paul wrote that apart from the
unrelenting external pressures he had to face, such as
persecution, hardship, and imprisonment, he also had
daily upon him the internal pressure "of concern for
all the churches" (2 Cor. 11:28). In spite of that, he
had room in his heart to feel the anxiety of others,

for he went on to write, "Who is weak without my being weak? Who is led into sin without my intense concern?" (v. 29). He wouldn't have had it any other way, though. In fact, that kind of response to pressure was what Paul looked for in those who would serve with him. Note how he commended Timothy to the Philippian church: "I have no one else of kindred spirit who will genuinely be concerned for your welfare" (Phil. 2:20; cf. 1 Cor. 4:17).

Anyone who knows and loves Jesus Christ is capable of handling pressure that way. The wrong way to handle the stresses of life is to worry about them. Jesus said three times, "Do not be anxious" (see Matt. 6:25, 31, 34). Paul later reiterated, "Be anxious for nothing" (Phil. 4:6). Worry at any time is a sin because it violates the clear biblical command.

We allow our daily concerns to turn into worry and therefore sin when our thoughts become focused on changing the future instead of doing our best to handle our present circumstances. Such thoughts are unproductive. They end up controlling us—though it should be the other way around—and cause us to neglect other responsibilities and relationships. That brings on legitimate feelings of guilt. If we don't deal with those feelings in a productive manner by getting back on track in life, we'll lose hope instead of finding answers. When left unresolved, worry can debilitate one's mind and body—and even lead to panic attacks.

To tackle worry and anxiety in a biblical fashion, first we need to know the primary Scripture passages on the topic. Then we need to consider those passages in their context, not merely cite and recite them unthinkingly or use them as props for a nice story or a suggested behavior-modifying technique. As a person "thinks within himself, so he is" (Prov. 23:7).

As we realign our thinking on anxiety with what God says about it in His Word and why, we will be different people. We will be ready to apply His precious Word to our hearts. We won't just know we're not to worry; we will have confidence and success in doing something about it. And we can be aggressive in our approach. I've titled this short book *Found: God's Peace* because I want you to know you can overcome your anxieties. If you would like to read a fuller study on the topic, my book *Anxious for Nothing* goes deeper. Otherwise, I trust you will find the content here practical and biblical, enabling you to say with the psalmist:

> When I said, "My foot is slipping," your love, O LORD, supported me. When anxiety was great within me, your consolation brought joy to my soul. (Ps. 94:18–19 NIV)

# Chapter 1

## AVOIDING ANXIETY
## THROUGH PRAYER

Just as Matthew 6 is Jesus's great statement on worry, Philippians 4 is the apostle Paul's charter on how to avoid anxiety. Those passages are the most comprehensive portions of Scripture dealing with our topic and therefore are foundational to understanding how God feels about anxiety and why He feels that way. The teaching is clear, compelling, and direct. In Philippians 4:6–9, Paul issued a series of commands:

Be anxious for nothing, but in everything by prayer and supplication with thanksgiving let your requests be made known to God. And the peace of God, which surpasses all comprehension, will guard your hearts and your minds in Christ Jesus.

Finally, brethren, whatever is true, whatever is honorable, whatever is right, whatever is pure, whatever is lovely, whatever is of good repute, if there is any excellence and if anything worthy of praise, dwell on these things. The things you have learned and received and heard and seen in me, practice these things, and the God of peace will be with you.

Paul straightaway said not to worry, but he doesn't leave us there. His instruction helps us fill the vacuum by directing us toward positive steps: right praying, right thinking, and right action. The best way to eliminate a bad habit is to replace it with a good one, and few habits are as bad as worrying.

The foremost way to avoid anxiety is through prayer. Right thinking and action are the next logical steps, but it all begins with prayer.

## React to Problems with Thankful Prayer

Paul said, "In everything by prayer and supplication with thanksgiving let your requests be made known to God" (Phil. 4:6). This teaching tells us how to pray with gratitude. The Greek terms Paul used refer to specific petitions made to God in the midst of difficulty.

Instead of praying to God with feelings of doubt, discouragement, or discontent, we are to approach Him with a thankful attitude before we utter even one word. We can do that with sincerity when we realize that God promises not to allow anything to happen to us that will be too much for us to bear (1 Cor. 10:13), and He promises to work out everything for our good in the end (Rom. 8:28) and to "perfect, confirm, strengthen and establish" us in the midst of our suffering (1 Peter 5:10).

These are key principles for living the Christian life. Go beyond memorizing them to letting them be the grid through which you automatically interpret all that happens to you. Know that all your difficulties are within God's purpose, and thank Him for His available power and promises.

Being thankful will release you from fear and worry. It is a tangible demonstration of trusting your situation to God's sovereign control. And it is easy to do, since there are so many blessings to be thankful for: knowing that God will supply all our needs (Phil. 4:19), that He stays closely in touch with our lives (Ps. 139:3), that He cares about us (1 Peter 5:7), that all power belongs to Him (Ps. 62:11), that He is making us more and more like Christ (Rom. 8:29; Phil. 1:6), and that no detail escapes Him (Ps. 147:5).

The prophet Jonah reacted with thankful prayer when a great fish swallowed him (Jon. 2:1, 9). If you suddenly found yourself swimming in a fish's gastric juices, how do you think you'd react? Maybe you'd cry out, "God, what are You doing? Where are You?

Why is this happening to me?" If there were ever an excuse for panic, surely this would be it. But no, Jonah reacted differently:

> I called out of my distress to the LORD,
> And He answered me....
> You had cast me into the deep,
> Into the heart of the seas....
> I have been expelled from Your sight....
> Water encompassed me to the point of death.
> The great deep engulfed me,
> Weeds were wrapped around my head.
> I descended to the roots of the mountains....
> While I was fainting away,
> I remembered the LORD,
> And my prayer came to You,
> Into Your holy temple.
> Those who regard vain idols
> Forsake their faithfulness,
> But I will sacrifice to You
> With the voice of thanksgiving....
> Salvation is from the LORD. (vv. 2–9)

Although Jonah had his weaknesses, he reflected profound spiritual stability in this prayer. He was confident of God's ability to deliver him if He so chose. In the same way the peace of God will help stabilize us if we react to our circumstances, however unusual or ordinary, with thankful prayer instead of anxiety. That's the promise of Philippians 4:7: "The peace of God, which surpasses all comprehension, will guard your hearts and your minds in Christ Jesus."

This precious verse promises inner calm and tranquility to believers who pray with a thankful attitude. Notice, however, it doesn't promise what the answer to our prayers will be.

This peace "surpasses all comprehension," which speaks of its divine origin. It transcends human intellect, analysis, and insight. No human counselor can give it to you because it's a gift from God in response to gratitude and trust.

The real challenge of Christian living is not to eliminate every uncomfortable circumstance from our lives, but to trust our sovereign, wise, good, and powerful God in the midst of every situation. Things that might trouble us, such as the way we look, the way others treat us, or where we live or work, can actually be sources of strength, not weakness.

Jesus said to His disciples, "These things I have spoken to you, so that in Me you may have peace. In the world you have tribulation, but take courage; I have overcome the world" (John 16:33). As disciples of Christ, we need to accept the fact that we live in an imperfect world and allow God to do His perfect work in us. Our Lord will give us His peace as we confidently entrust ourselves to His care.

The peace of God "will guard your hearts and your minds in Christ Jesus" (Phil. 4:7). John Bunyan's allegory *The Holy War* illustrates how this peace guards the believer's heart from anxiety, doubt, fear, and distress. In it, Mr. God's-Peace was appointed to guard the city of Mansoul. As long as Mr. God's-Peace ruled, Mansoul enjoyed harmony, happiness, joy, and health. However, Prince Emmanuel (Christ) went away because Mansoul grieved him. Consequently, Mr. God's-Peace resigned his commission, and chaos resulted.

The believer who doesn't live in the confidence of
God's sovereignty will lack God's peace and be left to
the chaos of a troubled heart. But our confident trust
in the Lord will allow us to thank Him in the midst of
trials because we have God's peace on duty to protect
our hearts.

During World War II, an armed German
freighter picked up a missionary whose ship had been
torpedoed. He was put in the hold. For a while he was
too terrified to even close his eyes. Sensing the need to
adjust his perspective, he told of how he got through
the night: "I began communing with the Lord. He
reminded me of His word in the 121st Psalm: 'My
help cometh from the LORD, which made heaven and
earth. He will not suffer thy foot to be moved: he that
keepeth thee will not slumber. Behold, he … shall
neither slumber nor sleep' (vv. 2–4 KJV).… So I said,
'Lord there isn't really any use for both of us to stay
awake tonight. If You are going to keep watch, I'll
thank Thee for some sleep!'"[1] He replaced his fear and
anxiety with thankful prayer, and the peace of God
that resulted enabled him to sleep soundly. You too

will enjoy peace and rest when you cultivate the habit of looking to God with a grateful attitude.

## Focus on Godly Virtues

Prayer is our chief means of avoiding anxiety. After Paul said not to be anxious (Phil. 4:6), he added two complete sentences specifying how we're to pray and what the benefits will be. The English text, reflective of the Greek, launches into a new paragraph on godly thinking and practices. Philippians 4 is often oversimplified and misrepresented as a mere grocery list on how to deal with worry, but it is much more than that. As believers, we're to leave the sin of worry behind with our prayers and gradually become different people through new ways of thinking and acting. Let's now explore these next steps beyond worry.

Paul wrote these words: "Whatever is true, whatever is honorable, whatever is right, whatever is pure, whatever is lovely, whatever is of good repute, if there is any excellence and if anything worthy of praise, dwell on these things" (Phil. 4:8). As mentioned earlier, we are the products of our thinking. According to

Proverbs 23:7, "As [a person] thinks within himself, so he is." Unfortunately, many psychologists believe we can find stability by recalling our past sins, hurts, and abuses. That kind of thinking has infiltrated Christianity. The apostle Paul, however, said to focus only on what is right and honorable, not on the sins of darkness (Eph. 5:11–13).

## How We Think

To give you some background, let's survey what Scripture says about our thinking patterns before, at, and after salvation.

Describing unredeemed humanity, Paul wrote: "As they did not see fit to acknowledge God any longer, God gave them over to a depraved mind" (Rom. 1:28). Once, our minds were corrupt. Worse, our minds were also blind, for "the god of this world has blinded the minds of the unbelieving" (2 Cor. 4:4). As a result, our minds were engaged in futile thoughts (Eph. 4:17). Indeed, prior to salvation, people's minds are "darkened in their understanding, excluded from the life of God because of the ignorance that is in them" (v. 18). Since the mind of the unbeliever is corrupt, it doesn't choose what is good; since it is spiritually blind, it doesn't know what is good; since its thoughts are futile, it doesn't perform what is good; and since it is ignorant, it doesn't even know what evil it is doing. What a tragic train of thought!

The ability to think clearly and correctly is a tremendous blessing from God. It all begins with the gospel, which is "the power of God for salvation" (Rom. 1:16). The Lord uses the gospel to illumine the mind of the unbeliever. In fact, Paul said that faith comes by hearing about Christ (Rom. 10:17). Salvation begins in the mind as an individual comes to realize the seriousness of sin and Christ's atoning work on his or her behalf. Jesus said, "You shall love the Lord your God with all your heart, and with all your soul, and with all your strength, and with all your mind" (Luke 10:27). Salvation requires an intelligent response: trust in the revealed truth of God, which proves itself in life to be true and reasonable.

Recall that Jesus said, "Look at the birds of the air, that they do not sow, nor reap nor gather into barns, and yet your heavenly Father feeds them. Are you not worth much more than they?" (Matt. 6:26). Martyn Lloyd-Jones, commenting on that verse, explained:

> Faith, according to our Lord's teaching … is primarily thinking…. We must spend more time in studying our Lord's lessons in observation and deduction. The Bible is full of logic, and we must never think of faith as something purely mystical. We do not just sit down in an armchair and expect marvelous things to happen to us. That is not Christian faith. Christian faith is essentially thinking. Look at the birds, think about them, and draw your deductions. Look at the grass, look at the lilies of the field, consider them….
>
> Faith, if you like, can be defined like this: It is a man insisting upon thinking

when everything seems determined to blud-
geon and knock him down.... The trouble
with the person of little faith is that, instead
of controlling his own thought, his thought
is being controlled by something else, and, as
we put it, he goes round and round in circles.
That is the essence of worry.... That is not
thought; that is the absence of thought, a
failure to think.[2]

Some people assume worry is the result of too
much thinking. Actually, it's the result of too little
thinking in the right direction. If you know who God
is and understand His purposes, promises, and plans,
it will help you not to worry.

Faith isn't psychological self-hypnosis or wishful
thinking, but a reasoned response to revealed truth.
When we in faith embrace Christ as our Lord and
Savior, our minds are transformed. The Holy Spirit is
at work in us, renewing us; and we receive a new mind
or way of thinking. Divine and supernatural thoughts
are injected into our human thought patterns.

"The thoughts of God no one knows except the Spirit of God," said Paul, but we as believers "have received, not the spirit of the world, but the Spirit who is from God, so that we may know the things freely given to us by God" (1 Cor. 2:11–12). In other words, because the Holy Spirit indwells us, the very thoughts of God are available to us.

Since we still live in a fallen world, however, our renewed minds need ongoing cleansing and refreshment. Jesus said that God's chief agent for purifying our thinking is His Word (John 15:3). Paul reiterated that concept many times:

- Romans 12:1–2: "Therefore I urge you, brethren, by the mercies of God, to present your bodies a living and holy sacrifice, acceptable to God, which is your spiritual service of worship. And do not be conformed to this world, but be transformed by the renewing of your mind, so that you may prove what the will of God is, that which is good and acceptable and perfect."

- Ephesians 4:23: "Be renewed in the spirit of your mind."
- Colossians 3:10: "Put on the new self who is being renewed to a true knowledge according to the image of the One who created him."
- 1 Thessalonians 5:21: "Examine everything carefully; hold fast to that which is good."

The New Testament calls us to the mental discipline of right thinking. Paul said, "Set your mind on the things above, not on the things that are on earth" (Col. 3:2). In addition, Peter said, "Prepare your minds for action, keep sober in spirit, fix your hope completely on the grace to be brought to you at the revelation of Jesus Christ" (1 Peter 1:13).

Think how often Paul said in his letters, "I would not … that ye should be ignorant" (Rom. 11:25; 1 Cor. 10:1; 2 Cor. 1:8; 1 Thess. 4:13 KJV) and "know ye not" (Rom. 6:3, 16; 1 Cor. 3:16; 2 Cor. 13:5 KJV). He was concerned that we think rightly. Jesus Himself often used the term translated "think"

to help His listeners have the right focus (Matt. 5:17;
18:12; 21:28; 22:42).

## What We Should Think About

What is that right focus? Dwelling on "whatever is
true ... honorable ... right ... pure ... lovely ... of
good repute" (Phil. 4:8).

### TRUTHFUL THINGS

We will find what is true in God's Word. Jesus said,
"Sanctify them in the truth; Your word is truth" (John
17:17; see also Ps. 119:151). The truth is also in Christ
Himself—"just as truth is in Jesus," said Paul (Eph.
4:21). Dwelling on what is true necessitates meditat-
ing on God's Word and "fixing our eyes on Jesus, the
author and perfecter of [our] faith" (Heb. 12:2).

### NOBLE THINGS

The Greek word that is translated "honorable" refers
to what is noble, dignified, and worthy of respect.
We are to dwell on whatever is worthy of awe and
adoration—the sacred as opposed to the profane.

## RIGHTEOUS THINGS

The term "right" speaks of righteousness. Our thoughts are to be in perfect harmony with the eternal, unchanging, divine standard of our Holy God as revealed in Scripture. Right thinking is always consistent with God's absolute holiness.

## PURE THINGS

"Pure" refers to something morally clean and undefiled. We are to dwell on what is clean, not soiled.

## GRACIOUS THINGS

The Greek term translated "lovely" occurs only here in the New Testament and means "pleasing" or "amiable." The implication is that we are to focus on whatever is kind or gracious.

## PRAISEWORTHY THINGS

"Honorable" predominantly refers to something worthy of veneration by believers, but "good repute" refers more to what is reputable in the world at large. This term includes universally praised virtues such as courage and respect for others.

In essence Paul was saying, "Since there are so many excellent and worthy things out there, please focus on them." Focusing on godly virtues will affect what you decide to see (such as television programs, books, or magazines) and say (perhaps to family and those at work). That's because your thinking affects your desires and behavior.

How does all that lofty teaching apply to fear and anxiety? Jay Adams gave this practical advice:

> Whenever you catch your mind wandering back into the forbidden territory (and you can be sure that it will—more frequently at first, until you retrain and discipline it …) change the direction of your thought. Do not allow yourself one conscious moment of such thought. Instead, crisply ask God to help you to refocus upon those things that fit into Paul's list recorded in Philippians 4:8–9. The attitude must grow within you that

says: "So if I have a fear experience, so what? It's unpleasant, it's disturbing, but I'll live through it—at least I always have before." When you honestly can think this way without becoming anxious, you will know that the change has been made.[3]

## Practice What's Been Preached

All this godly thinking is to lead to a practical end. Paul put it this way: "The things you have learned and received and heard and seen in me, practice these things, and the God of peace will be with you" (Phil. 4:9).

Paul's words speak of action that's repetitious or continuous. When we say someone is practicing the violin or something else, we mean that person is working to improve a skill. When we say a doctor or lawyer has a practice, we are referring to his or her professional routine. Similarly, the word here refers to one's pattern of life or conduct.

God's Word cultivates the godly attitudes, thoughts, and actions that will keep trials and temptations from overwhelming us. To understand the relationship between the three, consider this analogy: If a police officer sees someone who is about to violate the law, the officer will restrain that person. Similarly, godly attitudes and thoughts produced by the Word act as police officers to restrain the flesh before it commits a crime against the standard of God's Word. But if they aren't on duty, they can't restrain the flesh, and the flesh is free to violate the law of God.

Right attitudes and thoughts must precede right practices. Only spiritual weapons will help in our warfare against the flesh (2 Cor. 10:4). By avoiding anxiety through prayer and making other such attitude adjustments, we can take "every thought captive to the obedience of Christ" (v. 5).

Pure behavior, in turn, produces spiritual peace and stability. The prophet Isaiah said, "The work of righteousness will be peace, and the service of righteousness, quietness and confidence forever" (Isa. 32:17). Similarly, James wrote, "The wisdom from above is first pure, then peaceable.... The seed whose fruit is righteousness is sown in peace by those who make peace" (James 3:17–18).

Paul said, "The things you have learned and received and heard and seen in me, practice these things" (Phil. 4:9). Paul exemplified the spiritual fruit of peace, joy, humility, faith, and gratitude. He clearly dwelled on what was true, honorable, right, pure, lovely, and of good repute. Therefore, he wasn't embarrassed to tell people who knew him well to practice what they had seen in his life.

Today we have the New Testament as the divine pattern for our conduct. In no way does that mean, however, that those who currently preach, teach, and represent the New Testament are permitted to live any way they want. Even though none of us are apostles, our lives are to be worthy of imitation or we disqualify ourselves from the ministry. Moreover, as believers we are all to prove ourselves "doers of the word, and not merely hearers" (James 1:22). Never expose yourself to the ministry of someone whose lifestyle you can't respect.

Finally, "the God of peace will be with you," said Paul, who ended on this note because he was addressing the issue of spiritual stability in the midst of trials

(Phil. 4:9). It takes us full circle to our original point of avoiding anxiety through prayer. When we follow that practice, "the peace of God, which surpasses all comprehension, will guard [our] hearts and … minds in Christ Jesus" (v. 7). There's no better protection from worry than that.

# Chapter 2

## CASTING YOUR CARES ON GOD

The apostle Peter was a worrier. He worried about drowning when he was walking on water, even though Jesus was right there with him (Matt. 14:29–31). He worried about what was going to happen to Jesus in the garden of Gethsemane, so he pulled out his sword and tried to take on a battalion of Roman soldiers (John 18:2–3, 10)—worry is never smart! For another example, when Peter worried about Jesus being crucified, he *ordered* Jesus—God Almighty—not to go to the cross

(Matt. 16:22). That took some guts! Nevertheless, although Peter had ongoing trouble with anxiety, he learned how to deal with it. He passed this lesson on to us:

> Clothe yourselves with humility toward one another, for God is opposed to the proud, but gives grace to the humble. Therefore humble yourselves under the mighty hand of God, that He may exalt you at the proper time, casting all your anxiety on Him, because He cares for you. (1 Peter 5:5–7)

To establish the context for you, verses 5–14 are the final section of Peter's first epistle. It could well be titled "Fundamental Attitudes for Spiritual Maturity." I think every sincere Christian thinks to himself or herself, *I want to be spiritually mature. I want to be spiritually effective. I want to be all that God wants me to be.* It's good to have those desires, but the reality comes to pass only when you and I build our lives on certain fundamentals. The one we will focus on is humility, for only from humility comes the ability to truly hand over all our cares to God.

## Develop a Humble Attitude

Did you know that God has created a certain garment that fits everybody? When I was in New Orleans, I vividly recall an aggressive saleswoman who wouldn't leave me alone. She practically dragged me into her store, saying, "Why don't you come in? You might want to *buy* something." As I looked around, I observed that the only thing she sold was women's clothing. I said, "I have a basic rule: I don't buy women's clothes for me, and I don't buy women's clothes for my wife because I might get the wrong thing, especially since I'm out of town." She had a quick comeback: "Well, it doesn't matter. All these clothes fit everybody." I thought, *If I brought home something for my wife that could fit everybody, she wouldn't take it as a compliment!* Only one garment can be honestly advertised as one size fits all, and that is the garment of humility, which every believer is commanded to put on.

## Humility toward Others

When Peter said to "clothe yourselves with humility toward one another" (1 Peter 5:5), he had a specific image in mind. He used a Greek term that means to tie something on oneself with a knot or a bow. It came to refer especially to a work apron. Slaves would put on aprons over their clothes to keep them clean, just as you might do before you start a messy chore. The word became a synonym for humble service.

Humility is the attitude that you are not too good to serve others and that you are not too great to handle tasks that seem below you. Humility was not considered a virtue in the ancient world. Sadly, we have reverted to those times in this regard. Humble people today get mocked and trampled on. The world calls them wimps and instead exalts the proud. Although it was no different in Peter's day, he called us to be different.

In instructing us to put on the garment of a slave and serve others, Peter might have been thinking about his Lord. Recall the incident recorded in John 13, where Jesus "got up from supper, and laid aside

His garments; and taking a towel, He girded Himself. Then He poured water into the basin, and began to wash the disciples' feet and to wipe them with the towel with which He was girded" (vv. 4–5).

Here's the scene: The disciples were about to start supper with dirty feet. That was a problem because in the ancient Near East, people ate while reclining on floor mats. In a good-sized group, one person's head could be near another person's feet. It became customary for the lowliest person in the household to wash everyone's feet before the food was served.

Since none of the disciples volunteered to perform this servant duty, Jesus took on the task Himself, leaving us all with an example of humble service. We clothe ourselves with humility toward one another when we meet one another's needs without regarding any task as being beneath us. Don't wait for someone else to step in and do the dirty work.

Another instructive text is Philippians 2:3–5:

Do nothing from selfishness or empty conceit, but with humility of mind regard one

another as more important than yourselves;
do not merely look out for your own personal
interests, but also for the interests of others.
Have this attitude in yourselves which was
also in Christ Jesus.

Be warned: It's a challenge to regard someone
else as more important than yourself. Pride and selfishness dwell naturally within fallen human flesh.
Jesus again is our example to follow. Paul went on
to say how Christ at first existed in an exalted state
with the Father but then humbled Himself even
to the point of a shameful death that He might
serve us (Phil. 2:6–8). The first step to enjoying the
blessings of humility is to stoop to serve even the
unworthy.

## Humility toward God

To support his exhortation to clothe ourselves in
humility toward one another, Peter gave this citation
from the Old Testament: "God is opposed to the
proud but gives grace to the humble" (1 Peter 5:5; see

also Prov. 3:34 NIV). That verse provides keen motivation for displaying humility. We will be blessed if we are humble and chastised if we are not. As we will soon see, one of those blessings is the ability to deal with anxiety.

First, however, let's explore why God is opposed to the proud. Very simply, He hates pride. According to Proverbs 6:16, "There are six things which the LORD hates, yes, seven which are an abomination to Him." What is first on the list? "Haughty eyes" (v. 17), a visual depiction of pride. A few chapters later, wisdom personified declares, "The fear of the LORD is to hate evil; pride and arrogance and the evil way and the perverted mouth, I hate" (8:13).

God has a strong reason for hating pride so much; it is the sin that led to the fall of humanity, and it was the fatal flaw of the tempter who brought about such destruction. Pride is what prompted Lucifer to say in his heart:

I will ascend to heaven; I will raise my throne above the stars of God, and I will sit on the

mount of assembly in the recesses of the
north. I will ascend above the heights of
the clouds; I will make myself like the Most
High. (Isa. 14:13–14)

God's grace is reserved for the humble.

For thus says the high and exalted One who
lives forever, whose name is Holy, "I dwell
on a high and holy place, and also with the
contrite and lowly of spirit in order to revive
the spirit of the lowly and to revive the heart
of the contrite." (Isa. 57:15)

God lives in an exalted place. Who lives with
Him there? Not the high and mighty, but the lowly.

God concluded His message to Isaiah by saying,
"To this one I will look, to him who is humble and
contrite of spirit, and who trembles at My word"
(Isa. 66:2). He blesses the humble, and He opposes
the proud. I mourn to see people stumbling around
trying to fix their lives, to find some kind of solution,

some kind of book or therapy that will solve their problems, but find no deliverance. Instead of experiencing the grace of God, they experience the correcting hand of God because they are proud.

Peter's advice is: "Therefore humble yourselves under the mighty hand of God, that He may exalt you at the proper time" (1 Peter 5:6). After all, "He has told you, O man, what is good; and what does the LORD require of you but to do justice, to love kindness, and to walk humbly with your God?" (Mic. 6:8). The key is never to contest God's wisdom but instead to accept humbly whatever God brings into your life as coming from His hand.

"The mighty hand of God" is an Old Testament symbol of God's controlling power. The humble person realizes that God is in charge, always accomplishing His sovereign purposes. That realization, however, should not go so far as to produce the fatalistic attitude of crying uncle to God—for example, "God, You're too strong for me to contend with. No use battering my head against the walls of the universe." For over eight hundred years, perhaps no one

has portrayed that attitude more wrenchingly than
Omar Khayyám did in *The Rubáiyát*:

> *But helpless Pieces of the Game He plays*
> *Upon this Chequer-board of Nights and Days;*
> *Hither and thither moves, and checks, and slays,*
> *And one by one back in the Closet lays.*
>
> *The Ball no question makes of Ayes and Noes,*
> *But Here or There as strikes the Player goes;*
> *And He that toss'd you down into the Field,*
> *He knows about it all—He knows—HE knows!*
>
> *The Moving Finger writes; and, having writ,*
> *Moves on: nor all your Piety nor Wit*
> *Shall lure it back to cancel half a Line,*
> *Nor all your Tears wash out a Word of it.*
> *(stanzas LXIX–LXXI)*

Yes, God is all-powerful. Contrary to the fanci-
ful characters of some science-fiction shows, He is
the *only* omnipotent being. He is capable of doing

all Khayyám wrote about and more, but the balancing factor is that God cares about us. We will soon explore that truth in more detail.

In Scripture, the mighty hand of God's power means different things at different times. Sometimes it speaks of deliverance, as in the exodus of Israel from Egypt (Ex. 3:20). Sometimes it serves as a shield to protect the believer through a time of testing. Sometimes it is a chastening hand.

Let's look at a specific example from the book of Job. In the midst of terrible suffering, Job tragically compounded his anguish by doing what he should have learned never to do: He contested God's wisdom, expressly resenting what the mighty hand of God had brought him. Take time to sense the raw human emotion seething under the words of his lament:

> I cry out to you, O God, but you do not answer; I stand up, but you merely look at me. You turn on me ruthlessly; with the might of your hand you attack me. You snatch me up and drive me before the

wind; you toss me about in the storm. I know you will bring me down to death. (Job 30:20–23 NIV)

Perhaps Job was feeling like one of Khayyám's chess pieces. Here the mighty hand of God was not the hand of deliverance but of testing, acting as the refiner's fire to make Job's faith come out like gold. Contrary to Job's gloomy expectations, that's exactly what happened. Once God had humbled him, Job confessed, "Surely I spoke of things I did not understand, things too wonderful for me to know.… My ears had heard of you but now my eyes have seen you. Therefore I despise myself and repent in dust and ashes" (Job 42:3, 5–6 NIV). Job was saying, "God, now I see You as never before! I have learned that my perceptions are seriously limited, but now I know I can trust You implicitly."

Job's example is recorded for us, so we can learn the same lesson without having to go through the same struggles. Paul said, "Whatever was written in earlier times was written for our instruction, so that through perseverance and the encouragement of the Scriptures we might have hope" (Rom. 15:4). Never view the mighty hand of God in your life as a slap in the face; instead, see it as grounds for hope. Realize He has only good intentions toward you as His child, and therefore, expect to see good results from your present circumstances. Such an attitude leaves no steam on which worry can operate.

Peter said when you humble yourself under God's mighty hand, "He may exalt you at the proper time" (1 Peter 5:6). What's the proper time? His time, not our time. When will it be? When He has accomplished His purpose. Now that might seem a little vague, but there's no cause for concern: God has perfect timing. Indeed, our salvation depended on His perfect timing. Paul specified that the hope of eternal life was "at the proper time manifested" through Jesus Christ (Titus 1:2–3). Trusting in God's timing is no light or peripheral matter to the Christian faith.

At the proper time God will exalt us. Paul used a Greek term that speaks of lifting us out of our present trouble. For the Christian, even the worst trial is only temporary. *Remember that*, for you *will* be tempted to conclude that because there is no end in sight, there is no end at all. Don't believe it for a minute; God promises to lift you out.[1]

How are we to conduct ourselves until the promised time of deliverance? Peter said, "Humble yourselves … casting all your anxiety on Him, because He cares for you" (1 Peter 5:6–7).

## Learn to Trust

Humility requires strong confidence in a caring God. I can't humble myself under God's pressure if I don't think He cares, but I can if I know He does. Peter said to have an attitude of trust. The basis of that trust is the loving care God has repeatedly shown us. You cast your anxiety on Him when you're able to say, however haltingly, "Lord, it's difficult.… I'm having trouble handling this trial, but I'm giving You the whole deal because I know You care for me."

The word translated "casting" in 1 Peter 5:7 was used to describe throwing something on something else, such as a blanket over a pack animal (e.g., Luke

19:35). Take all your anxiety—all the discontent, discouragement, despair, questioning, pain, and suffering that you're going through—and toss it all onto God. Trade it in for trust in God, who really cares about you.

Hannah is a great illustration of someone who did just that. She didn't have any children, which was a significant trial for a Jewish woman in ancient times. The book of 1 Samuel tells us what she did about her problem:

> She, greatly distressed, prayed to the LORD and wept bitterly. She made a vow and said, "O LORD of hosts, if You will indeed look on the affliction of Your maidservant and remember me, and not forget Your maidservant, but will give Your maidservant a son, then I will give him to the LORD all the days of his life.…"
>
> Now it came about, as she continued praying before the LORD, that Eli [the priest] was watching her mouth. As for Hannah,

she was speaking in her heart, only her lips were moving, but her voice was not heard. So Eli thought she was drunk. Then Eli said to her, "How long will you make yourself drunk? Put away your wine from you." But Hannah replied, "No, my lord, I am a woman oppressed in spirit; I have drunk neither wine nor strong drink, but I have poured out my soul before the LORD. Do not consider your maidservant as a worthless woman, for I have spoken until now out of my great concern and provocation." Then Eli answered and said, "Go in peace; and may the God of Israel grant your petition that you have asked of Him." She said, "Let your maidservant find favor in your sight." So the woman went her way and ate, and her face was no longer sad. (1:10–18)

What happened to her? Why was she no longer sad? Her circumstances hadn't changed, but *she changed* when she cast her cares on the Lord. Soon thereafter, God blessed her with a son, Samuel, who grew to be a great man of God. God also gave her three other sons and two daughters. Hannah is proof that when you remain humble under the mighty hand of God, casting all your anxiety on His loving care, He will exalt you in due time.

I have no doubt that Peter had Psalm 55:22 in mind when he wrote his first epistle: "Cast your burden upon the LORD and He will sustain you; He will never allow the righteous to be shaken." Now that doesn't mean we will feel stable and secure all the time. Think how Hannah felt when the priest accused her of being drunk. Sometimes when we're bearing burdens that in themselves seem too great to bear, people treat us insensitively and heap more burdens on us. But, like Hannah, we can be gracious about it and find relief through prayer to the God who does care.

If you need to be reminded now and then that God really cares about you, remember what Jesus said in the Sermon on the Mount: Since He luxuriously arrays mere field lilies, don't you think He will clothe you? Since He faithfully feeds mere birds, don't you think He will feed you? Spiritual maturity begins with these fundamentals: an attitude of humility toward God and others and trust in God's care.

What will that attitude of trust look like when dealing with fear and anxiety? We go again to Jay Adams for some practical advice:

> Stop trying to stop fearing [or worrying]. Say to God in your own words (and mean it) something like this: "Lord, if I have another [bout with fear or worry], I'll just have to have it. I am going to leave that in your hands." That is something of what Peter meant when he wrote: "Casting all of your care upon Him for He cares for you" (1 Peter 5:7). Then, make your plans and go ahead and do whatever God holds you responsible for doing. Fill your mind with concern for the other persons toward whom you are expressing love and how you will do so, in whatever you are doing.[2]

A prayer found in a small devotional manual that first appeared in Europe over five hundred years ago prepares us to follow through with that advice. The manual is attributed to Thomas à Kempis and is titled *The Imitation of Christ*:

> O Lord ... greater is Thy anxiety for me (Matt. 6:30; John 6:20), than all the care that I can take for myself. For he standeth but very totteringly, who casteth not all his anxiety upon Thee. (1 Peter 5:7)
>
> O Lord, if only my will may remain right and firm towards Thee, do with me whatsoever it shall please Thee. For it cannot be anything but good, whatsoever Thou shalt do with me. If Thou willest me to be in darkness, be Thou blessed; and if Thou willest me to be in light, be Thou again blessed. If Thou vouchsafe to comfort me, be Thou blessed; and if Thou willest me to be afflicted, be Thou ever equally blessed.[3]

# Chapter 3

## HAVING PEACE IN EVERY CIRCUMSTANCE

Paul closed his first letter to the Thessalonians with practical instructions on ministering to problem people in the church, including the worried. In this chapter, we will see how he closed his second letter to them—with a prayer any anxious Christian would love someone to have prayed on his or her behalf: "May the Lord of peace Himself continually grant you peace in every circumstance.... The grace of our Lord Jesus Christ be with you" (2 Thess. 3:16, 18).

## A Prayer for God's Peace

Peace is commonly defined as the sense of calm, tranquility, quietness, bliss, contentment, and well-being we feel when everything is going the way we'd like it to go. That definition, however, is incomplete because that feeling can be produced also by a pill—or by alcohol, a nap, a generous inheritance, or even deliberate deception. The reassurance of a friend or someone you love whispering sweet nothings into your ear can also give you that type of peace.

That's not the kind of peace Paul had in mind. Godly peace has nothing to do with human beings or human circumstances. In fact, godly peace cannot be produced on a human level at all. Any peace that humans can produce is very fragile. It can be destroyed instantly by failure, doubt, fear, difficulty, guilt, shame, distress, regret, sorrow, the anxiety of making a wrong choice, the anticipation of being mistreated or victimized by someone, the uncertainty of the future, and any challenge to our position or possessions. And we experience these things daily.

The peace that God gives is not subject to the vicissitudes of life. It is a spiritual peace; it is an attitude of heart and mind when we believe and thus know deep down that all is well between ourselves and God. Along with it is the assurance that He is lovingly in control of everything. We as Christians should know for sure that our sins are forgiven, that God is concerned with our well-being, and that heaven is our destiny. God's peace is our possession and privilege by divine right. Let's first consider its origin.

## It Is Divine

This peace is defined for us in several ways in 2 Thessalonians 3:16. To begin with, it is divine: "May the Lord of peace *Himself* … grant you peace." The Lord of peace is the one who gives it. The pronoun "Himself" is emphatic in the Greek text and underscores God's personal involvement. Christian peace, the peace unique to Christians, comes personally from Him. It is the very essence of His nature.

To put it simply, peace is an attribute of God. If I asked you to list the attributes of God, these are the ones that would probably come most readily to mind: His love, grace, mercy, justice, holiness, wisdom, truth, omnipotence, immutability, and immortality. But do you ever think of God as being characterized by peace? In fact, He is peace. Whatever it is that He gives us, He has and He is. There is no lack of perfect peace in His being. God is never stressed. He is never anxious. He never worries. He never doubts. He never fears. God is never at cross-purposes with Himself. He never has problems making up His mind.

God lives in perfect calm and contentment. Why? Because He's in charge of everything and can operate everything perfectly according to His will. Since He is omniscient, He is never surprised. Nothing can threaten His omnipotence. No possible sin can stain His holiness. Even His wrath is clear, controlled, and confident. There is no regret in His mind; for He has never done, said, or thought anything that He would change in any way.[1]

God enjoys perfect harmony within Himself. Our Bibles call Him "the Lord of peace," but in the Greek text a definite article appears before the word translated "peace," meaning He literally is "the Lord of *the peace*." This is real peace—the divine kind—not the kind the world has. Paul's prayer is that we might experience that kind of peace. Its source is God and God alone.

## It Is a Gift

Not only is this peace divine in origin, but it is also a gift. When Paul prayed, "Now may the Lord of peace Himself continually grant you peace," the word translated "grant" is the verb meaning "to give." It speaks of a gift. God's peace is a sovereign, gracious gift given to those who believe in the Lord Jesus Christ.

In Psalm 85:8, a verse you may have never noticed before, the psalmist stated, "I will hear what God the LORD will say; for He will speak peace to His people, to His godly ones." God grants peace to those who belong to Him. Jesus said, "My peace I give to you; not as the world gives do I give to you. Do not let your heart be troubled, nor let it be fearful" (John 14:27). There's no greater gift for the anxious than God's peace.

Some, however, will seek relief for their anxieties through a false peace. God is generous to whom He grants His peace, but there is a limit. Isaiah wrote, "'Peace, peace to him who is far and to him who is near,' says the LORD, 'and I will heal him.' But the wicked are like the tossing sea, for it cannot be quiet, and its waters toss up refuse and mud. 'There is no peace,' says my God, 'for the wicked'" (Isa. 57:19–21). He will grant peace to those who come to Him from near and far—those who grew up hearing much about Him and those who heard little to nothing—but those who don't come to Him, the wicked, enjoy no real peace.

Thomas Watson explained further:

Peace flows from sanctification, but they being unregenerate, have nothing to do with peace.... They may have a truce, but no peace. God may forebear the wicked a while, and stop the roaring of his cannon; but though there be a truce, yet there is no peace. The wicked may have something which looks

like peace, but it is not. They may be fear-
less and stupid; but there is a great difference
between a stupefied conscience, and a paci-
fied conscience.… This is the devil's peace; he
rocks men in the cradle of security; he cries,
Peace, peace, when men are on the precipice
of hell. The seeming peace a sinner has, is not
from the knowledge of his happiness, but the
ignorance of his danger.[2]

The peace of the wicked is born of delusion. True
peace is the child of saving grace. In a prayer similar to the one that closes 2 Thessalonians, Paul said,
"May the God of hope fill you with all joy and peace
in believing" (Rom. 15:13). Peace is a gift to those
who believe.

## It Is Always Available

God's peace is the gift that keeps on giving. Another
way to express that truth is how Paul said it: "May the
Lord of peace Himself continually grant you peace"
(2 Thess. 3:16). By adding "continually," Paul was

emphasizing that it is constantly available. The impli-cation is, however, that it can be interrupted.

It isn't God who interrupts our spiritual peace, but us. We can suspend the flow of peace in our lives by giving in to our flesh, which is still part of this world. Unless we "walk by the Spirit," our means of controlling the flesh (Gal. 5:16), we are open season to all kinds of anxieties: the dread of the unknown, the fear of disease and death—and we all can list a string of others. This unfortunate process begins when we stop focusing on our permanent condition in Christ, who will certainly bring us into His glory, and when we start basing our happiness on the fleeting things of the world. Thus, if we continue to rely on worldly things, which by definition will always change, we will spend our lives in distress.

People who can ride through the toughest issues of life and remain calm are not indifferent; they're just trusting God. What if our ride is a little bumpy? What if we're feeling troubled, anxious, and fearful? How can we restore the peace? How can it remain uninterrupted?

The psalmist said to himself, "Why are you in despair, O my soul? And why have you become disturbed within me? Hope in God, for I shall yet praise Him, the help of my countenance and my God" (Ps. 42:11). He reminded himself that God was there to help him. We can trust God because He is trustworthy. He genuinely cares for us.

Long ago, God made it perfectly clear to Israel that peace comes from obeying His Word (Lev. 26:1–6). The same truth applies today. Peace is restored through obedience. The first step is to turn away from sin. Sometimes the sin is the doubt, fear, or anxiety itself, but also it can be an underlying sin that has produced those feelings. Probe your heart and isolate the cause of its unrest. Give up the sin that has been revealed to you and obey God by applying the opposite virtue. In the case of anxiety, that means having faith in God to help you manage life's details.

Something else that will restore your peace is to accept whatever stresses or challenges God has seen fit to bring into your life. In the book of Job we read:

> Behold, how happy is the man whom God
> reproves,

So do not despise the discipline of the Almighty.
For He inflicts pain, and gives relief;
He wounds, and His hands also heal....
In famine He will redeem you from death,
And in war from the power of the sword.
You will be hidden from the scourge of the tongue,
And you will not be afraid of violence when
      it comes.
You will laugh at violence and famine,
And you will not be afraid of wild beasts.
For you will be in league with the stones of
      the field,
And the beasts of the field will be at peace
      with you.
You will know that your tent is secure,
For you will visit your abode and fear no loss.
    (5:17–18, 20–24)

If you understand that God is using all the difficulties you face to perfect you, you'll be at peace. It is not all for nothing. You may not always know why you're going through this or that, but be encouraged that there is a good reason. Turning to the New Testament, Paul said that if you want peace, do good (Rom. 2:10). All who do good will enjoy peace. To be more specific, "the wisdom from above is first pure, then peaceable…. And the seed whose fruit is righteousness is sown in peace by those who make peace" (James 3:17–18). Living according to the Word—according to heavenly wisdom, to God's revealed standard of righteousness—brings peace.

If you've lost God's peace in your life, you can find it again. Retrace your steps by trusting God in everything, turning away from sin and walking in obedience, enduring His refining work in your life, doing what is good, and living by the Word of God in a righteous way. As Paul said, God's peace is continually available to you. Avail yourself of it.

## It Is Not Subject to Circumstances

A final characteristic of God's peace is that it is not subject to circumstances. Paul's prayer was that we might continually enjoy it "in every circumstance" (2 Thess. 3:16). This peace is not subject to anything that happens in the worldly realm. It is not built on any human relationship. It is not built on any human circumstance. Rather, it is built on an unchanging divine relationship and a divine plan and promise from an unfailing God who will secure you in Himself and who will do everything for your good. This peace is unbreakable, unassailable, transcendent.

As we noted earlier, Jesus said, "Peace I leave with you; My peace I give to you; not as the world gives do I give to you. Do not let your heart be troubled, nor let it be fearful" (John 14:27). He was saying, "There's nothing to fear or be anxious about because I'm giving you a transcendent peace that—unlike the world's peace—is unassailable by any human circumstance." We demonstrate that Jesus keeps His promises when we remain calm in the midst of worldly upheavals that would normally tear us up and trouble our lives.

## A Prayer for God's Grace

Paul's great desire was that we enjoy that kind of well-being, which is why he prayed toward that end. His parting wish was this: "The grace of our Lord Jesus

Christ be with you all" (2 Thess. 3:18). He wanted every man and woman who would ever put his or her faith in Christ to experience the abiding presence of God's grace.

Grace is God's goodness or benevolence given to those who don't deserve it. "Grace and truth were realized through Jesus Christ" (John 1:17). It was in the person of God's Son that "the grace of God has appeared," making salvation available to all (Titus 2:11). Once we embrace this saving grace through faith in Christ, we are blessed with God's grace, enabling us to withstand any difficulty that would tend to make us anxious. Paul described this grace while confessing to a difficulty that brought him great anxiety:

> There was given me a thorn in the flesh, a messenger of Satan to torment me.... Concerning this I implored the Lord three times that it might leave me. And He has said to me, "My grace is sufficient for you, for power is perfected in weakness." Most gladly,

therefore, I will rather boast about my weaknesses, so that the power of Christ may dwell in me. Therefore I am well content with weaknesses, with insults, with distresses, with persecutions, with difficulties, for Christ's sake; for when I am weak, then I am strong. (2 Cor. 12:7–10)

As believers, we also are blessed with the grace that equips us for divine service. Paul expressed his appreciation for this grace in saying, "I thank Christ Jesus our Lord, who has strengthened me, because He considered me faithful, putting me into service, even though I was formerly a blasphemer and a persecutor and a violent aggressor. Yet I was shown mercy;… the grace of our Lord was more than abundant" (1 Tim. 1:12–14).

Grace is what enables us to grow spiritually in the knowledge of our Lord and Savior Jesus Christ (2 Peter 3:18). In the material realm, Paul appealed to God's grace in encouraging the Corinthian church to be generous in giving to the Lord's work: "God is able to make all grace abound to you, so that always having all sufficiency in everything, you may have an abundance for every good deed" (2 Cor. 9:8).

God's grace saves us, helps us cope with our anxieties, equips us for service, and enables us to grow spiritually and to be rich in God. Similar to God's peace, it is always available, and there is no limit to it. And again, similar to God's peace, the conditions for receiving it are trusting God, turning from sin, enduring the refining process, doing good, and living by the Word. As we are what we ought to be, God infuses us with His peace and grace. And that has a wonderful way of crowding out anxiety.

I want to end this chapter on a personal note. A few days after presenting *this very message* to my congregation at Grace Church, I had an unprecedented opportunity to apply it to my own life: I was notified that my wife and youngest daughter were in a serious automobile accident and that my wife, Patricia, would probably die. Everything seemed like a blur to me, the details frustratingly sketchy—I was afraid she was already dead. During my hour-long drive to the hospital, I had a lot of time to reflect on the severity of the situation. Yet I experienced a deep and settled peace simply because I knew God had not failed me—His grace was at work in my family's lives, and He was in complete control. I am happy to report that God spared both their lives and that Patricia recovered beautifully.

If you too rely on God's grace, He will see you through the most difficult trials.

# PSALMS FOR THE ANXIOUS

These excerpts from the Psalms are especially intended to attack anxiety. They movingly express and offer counsel in dealing with anxious thoughts and feelings we *all* have experienced. To derive the most benefit from this collection, you may want to scan them in one sitting and put a pencil mark by the ones that most closely relate to you. Go back and carefully read all the passages you marked, perhaps from several different Bible versions. Out of those, narrow down your list even further to the few that minister to you the most, and over time examine them in their entire context. To help you in your in-depth study, have on hand a good commentary on the Psalms, such as Charles Spurgeon's *The Treasury of David* (multiple volumes), or my book on this topic, *Anxious for Nothing*.

## Psalm 3

You are a shield around me, O LORD; you bestow glory on me and lift up my head. *To the LORD I cry aloud, and he answers me* from his holy hill. *I lie down and sleep; I wake again, because the LORD sustains me. I will not fear....* Arise, O LORD! Deliver me, O my God! (vv. 3–7 NIV)

## Psalm 4

Answer me when I call, O God of my righteousness! *You have relieved me in my distress*; be gracious to me and hear my prayer.... But know that the LORD has set apart the godly man for Himself; the LORD hears when I call to Him. Tremble, and do not sin; meditate in your heart upon your bed, and be still. Offer the sacrifices of righteousness, and trust in the LORD. Many are saying, "Who will show us any good?" Lift up the light of Your countenance upon us, O LORD! You have put gladness in my heart, more than when their grain and new wine abound. *In peace I will both lie down and sleep*, for You alone, O LORD, make me to dwell in safety. (vv. 1, 3–8)

## Psalm 5

Give ear to my words, O LORD, consider my meditation. *Hearken unto the voice of my cry*, my King, and my God: for unto thee will I pray. My voice shalt thou hear in the morning, O LORD; in the morning will I direct my prayer unto thee, and will look up.... *Let all those that put their trust in thee rejoice*: let them ever shout for joy, because thou defendest them: let them also that love thy name be joyful in thee. For thou, LORD, wilt bless the righteous; with favour wilt thou compass him as with a shield. (vv. 1–3, 11–12 KJV)

## Psalm 7

O LORD my God, *I take refuge in you*; save and deliver me.... My shield is God Most High, who saves the upright in heart.... I will give thanks to the LORD because of his righteousness and will sing praise to the name of the LORD Most High. (vv. 1, 10, 17 NIV)

## Psalm 11

*In the LORD I take refuge.* How then can you say to me: "Flee like a bird to your mountain.... When the foundations are being destroyed, what can the righteous do?" (vv. 1, 3 NIV)

## Psalm 16

*Keep me safe, O God,* for in you I take refuge. I said to the LORD, "You are my Lord; apart from you I have no good thing." ... LORD, you have assigned me my portion and my cup; you have made my lot secure.... I will praise the LORD, who counsels me; even at night my heart instructs me. *I have set the LORD always before me. Because he is at my right hand, I will not be shaken.* Therefore my heart is glad and my tongue rejoices; my body also will rest secure.... You have made known to me the path of life; you will fill me with joy in your presence, with eternal pleasures. (vv. 1–2, 5, 7–9, 11 NIV)

## Psalm 18

I love You, O LORD, my strength. The LORD is my rock and my fortress and my deliverer, my God, my rock, in whom I take refuge…. *The cords of death encompassed me*, and the torrents of ungodliness terrified me…. In my distress I called upon the LORD, and … my cry for help … came into His ears…. He sent from on high, He took me; He drew me out of many waters…. He brought me forth also into a [spacious] place; He rescued me, because He delighted in me…. You light my lamp; *the LORD my God illumines my darkness*. For by You I can run upon a troop; and by my God I can leap over a wall. As for God, His way is blameless; the word of the LORD is [flawless]; … *He is a shield to all who take refuge in Him*…. He makes my feet like hinds' feet, and sets me upon my high places…. The LORD lives, and blessed be my rock; and exalted be the God of my salvation. (vv. 1–2, 4, 6, 16, 19, 28–30, 33, 46)

## Psalm 23

*The LORD is my shepherd*; I shall not want. He maketh me to lie down in green pastures: he leadeth me beside the still waters. *He restoreth my soul*: he leadeth me in the paths of righteousness for his name's sake. Yea, though I walk through the valley of the shadow of death, I will fear no evil: for thou art with me; *thy rod and thy staff they comfort me*.... Surely goodness and mercy shall follow me all the days of my life: and I will dwell in the house of the Lord for ever. (vv. 1–4, 6 KJV)

## Psalm 25

To You, O Lord, I lift up my soul. O my God, in You I trust, do not let me be ashamed.... Indeed, none of those who wait for You will be ashamed.... Make me know Your ways, O Lord; teach me Your paths. Lead me in Your truth and teach me, for You are the God of my salvation; for You I wait all the day.... Do not remember the sins of my youth or my transgressions; according to Your lovingkindness remember me, for Your goodness' sake, O Lord.... My eyes are continually toward the Lord, for He will pluck my feet out of the net. *Turn to me and be gracious to me, for I am lonely and afflicted.* The troubles of my heart are enlarged; *bring me out of my distresses.* Look upon my affliction and my trouble…. Guard my soul and deliver me … for I take refuge in You. (vv. 1–5, 7, 15–18, 20)

## Psalm 27
Wait on the LORD: be of good courage, and *he shall strengthen thine heart.* (v. 14 KJV)

## Psalm 28
To you I call, O LORD my Rock; *do not turn a deaf ear to me.…* Praise be to the LORD, for he has heard my cry for mercy. The LORD is my strength and my shield; *my heart trusts in him, and I am helped.* My heart leaps for joy and I will give thanks to him in song. (vv. 1, 6–7 NIV)

## Psalm 31
In you, O LORD, I have taken refuge; let me never be put to shame…. Turn your ear to me, come quickly to my rescue; be my rock of refuge, a strong fortress to save me…. Into your hands I commit my spirit.…

I will be glad and rejoice in your love, for *you saw my affliction and knew the anguish of my soul.*... Be merciful to me, O LORD, for I am in distress; my eyes grow weak with sorrow, my soul and my body with grief. My life is consumed by anguish and my years by groaning; my strength fails because of my affliction, and my bones grow weak.... But I trust in you, O LORD; I say, "You are my God." *My times are in your hands.*... Be strong and take heart, all you who hope in the LORD. (vv. 1–2, 5, 7, 9–10, 14–15, 24 NIV)

## Psalm 34

I sought the LORD, and he answered me; *he delivered me from all my fears. Those who look to him are radiant;* their faces are never covered with shame. This poor man called, and the LORD heard him; he saved him out of all his troubles. The angel of the LORD encamps around those who fear him, and he delivers them.... The righteous cry out, and the LORD hears them; he delivers them from all their troubles. *The LORD is close to the brokenhearted and saves those who are crushed in spirit. A righteous man may have many troubles, but the LORD delivers him from them all.* (vv. 4–7, 17–19 NIV)

## Psalm 37

*Do not fret.…* Trust in the LORD and do good.… Delight yourself in the LORD and he will give you the desires of your heart. Commit your way to the LORD; trust in him and he will … make your righteous- ness shine like the dawn, the justice of your cause like the noonday sun. Be still before the LORD and wait patiently for him.… *Do not fret—it leads only to evil.…* The LORD upholds the righteous … [whose steps he has made] firm; though he stumble, he will not fall, for the LORD upholds him with his hand.… The LORD loves the just and will not forsake his faith- ful ones.… He is their stronghold in time of trouble. (vv. 1, 3–8, 17, 23–24, 28, 39 NIV)

## Psalm 46

*God is our refuge and strength, a very present help in trouble.* Therefore will not we fear, though the earth be removed.... Be still, and know that I am God. (vv. 1–2, 10 KJV)

## Psalm 54

Save me, O God, by your name; vindicate me by your might. Hear my prayer, O God; listen to the words of my mouth.... *Surely God is my help; the Lord is the one who sustains me....* For he has delivered me from all my troubles. (vv. 1–2, 4, 7 NIV)

## Psalm 56

When I am afraid, I will trust in you. In God, whose word I praise, *in God I trust; I will not be afraid....* You have delivered me from death and my feet from stumbling, that I may walk before God in the light of life. (vv. 3–4, 13 NIV)

## Psalm 61

Hear my cry, O God; attend unto my prayer. From the end of the earth will I cry unto thee, when my heart is overwhelmed: *lead me to the rock that is higher than I.* (vv. 1–2 KJV)

## Psalm 62

*My soul finds rest in God alone*; my salvation comes from him. He alone is my rock and my salvation; he is my fortress, I will never be shaken. (vv. 1–2 NIV)

## Psalm 68

Praise be to the Lord, to God our Savior, who daily bears our burdens. Our God is a God who saves; from the Sovereign LORD comes escape from death. (vv. 19–20 NIV)

## Psalm 70

Make haste, O God, to deliver me; *make haste to help me, O LORD....* Let all those that seek thee rejoice and be glad in thee: and let such as love thy salvation say continually, Let God be magnified. (vv. 1, 4 KJV)

## Psalm 84

Blessed are those whose strength is in you, who have set their hearts on pilgrimage.... They go from strength to strength, till each appears before God.... *The LORD God is a sun and shield*; the LORD bestows

favor and honor; no good thing does he with-
hold from those whose walk is blameless. O LORD
Almighty, blessed is the man who trusts in you. (vv.
5, 7, 11–12 NIV)

## Psalm 86

Hear, O LORD, and answer me, for *I am poor and
needy*. Guard my life, for I am devoted to you. You are
my God; save your servant who trusts in you. Have
mercy on me, O Lord, for *I call to you all day long*.
Bring joy to your servant, for to you, O Lord, I lift up
my soul. (vv. 1–4 NIV)

## Psalm 91

He who dwells in the shelter of the Most High will
rest in the shadow of the Almighty. I will say of the
LORD, "He is my refuge and my fortress, my God,
in whom I trust." … *"Because he loves me," says the
LORD, "I will rescue him*; I will protect him, for he
acknowledges my name. He will call upon me, and I
will answer him; I will be with him in trouble, I will
deliver him and honor him." (vv. 1–2, 14–15 NIV)

## Psalm 94

When I said, "My foot is slipping," your love, O LORD, supported me. *When anxiety was great within me, your consolation brought joy to my soul....* The LORD has become my fortress, and my God the rock in whom I take refuge. (vv. 18–19, 22 NIV)

## Psalm 102

Hear my prayer, O LORD; let my cry for help come to you. Do not hide your face from me when I am in distress. Turn your ear to me; when I call, answer me quickly.... *My heart is blighted and withered like grass; I forget to eat my food.* Because of my loud groaning I am reduced to skin and bones.... I lie awake ... because of your great wrath, for you have taken me up and thrown me aside.... [But the Lord] will respond to the prayer of the destitute; he will not despise their plea. (vv. 1–2, 4–5, 7, 10, 17 NIV)

## Psalm 112

Blessed is the man who fears the LORD, who finds great delight in his commands.... Surely he will never be shaken; a righteous man will be remembered forever. *He will have no fear of bad news; his heart is steadfast,* trusting in the LORD. His heart is secure, he will have no fear. (vv. 1, 6–8 NIV)

## Psalm 118

From my distress I called upon the LORD; the LORD answered me and set me in a large place. *The LORD is for me; I will not fear; what can man do to me?*... It is better to take refuge in the LORD than to trust in man.... You pushed me violently so that I was falling, but the LORD helped me. The LORD is my strength and song, and He has become my salvation.... I will not die, but live, and tell of the works of the LORD. *The LORD has disciplined me severely, but He has not given me over to death.* (vv. 5–6, 8, 13–14, 17–18)

## Psalm 120

I call on the LORD in my distress, and he answers me. (v. 1 NIV)

## Psalm 121

I will lift up mine eyes unto the hills, from whence cometh my help. My help cometh from the LORD, [who] made heaven and earth.... He will not let your foot slip.... The LORD watches over you.... [He] will keep you from all harm—he will watch over your life; the LORD will watch over your coming and going both now and forevermore. (vv. 1–2 KJV; vv. 3, 5, 7–8 NIV)

## Psalm 126

*He who goes out weeping,* carrying seed to sow, *will return with songs of joy,* carrying sheaves with him. (v. 6 NIV)

## Psalm 138

When I called, you answered me; you made me bold and stouthearted.... Though the LORD is on high, he looks upon the lowly.... *Though I walk in the midst of trouble, you preserve my life....* The LORD will fulfill his purpose for me; your love, O LORD, endures forever. (vv. 3, 6–8 NIV)

## Psalm 139

O LORD, you have searched me and you know me.... You perceive my thoughts from afar.... You are familiar with all my ways. Before a word is on my tongue you know it completely, O LORD.... Where can I go from your Spirit? Where can I flee from your presence? ... If I rise on the wings of the dawn, if I settle on the far side of the sea, even there your hand will guide me, your right hand will hold me fast.... You created my inmost being.... I praise you because I am fearfully and wonderfully made; your works are wonderful, I know that full well.... All the days ordained for me were written in your book before one of them came to be.... *Search me, O God, and know my heart; test me and know my anxious thoughts.* See if there is any offensive way in me, and lead me in the way everlasting. (vv. 1–4, 7, 9–10, 13–14, 16, 23–24 NIV)

## Psalm 142

How I plead with God, how I implore his mercy, pouring out my troubles before him. For *I am overwhelmed and desperate*, and you alone know which way I ought to turn. (vv. 1–3 TLB)

## Psalm 145

*The* LORD upholds all those who fall and *lifts up all who are bowed down.* The eyes of all look to you, and you give them their food at the proper time.… The LORD is near to all who call on him … in truth. (vv. 14–15, 18 NIV)

## Psalm 147

How good it is to sing praises to our God, how pleasant and fitting to praise him!… *He heals the brokenhearted and binds up their wounds.*… Great is our Lord and mighty in power; his understanding has no limit. The LORD sustains the humble.… [He] delights in those who … put their hope in his unfailing love. (vv. 1, 3, 5–6, 11 NIV)

# NOTES

## Introduction

1. Marian V. Liautaud, *Today's Christian Woman*, July/August 1991, 24.

## Chapter 1: Avoiding Anxiety through Prayer

1. Paul S. Rees, *The Adequate Man: Paul in Philippians* (Westwood, NJ: Revell, 1959), 106.

2. D. Martyn Lloyd-Jones, *The Sermon on the Mount*, vol. 2 (Grand Rapids, MI: Eerdmans, 1960), 129–30.

3. Jay E. Adams, *What Do You Do When Fear Overcomes You?* (Phillipsburg, NJ: P&R Publishing Company, 1975).

## Chapter 2: Casting Your Cares on God

1. For more on this subject, read John MacArthur, *Standing Strong: How to Resist the Enemy of Your Soul*, 3rd ed. (Colorado Springs: David C Cook, 2012).

2. Jay E. Adams, *What Do You Do When Fear Overcomes You?* (Phillipsburg, NJ: P&R Publishing Company, 1975).

3. Thomas à Kempis, *The Imitation of Christ*, trans. Geoffrey Cumberlege (New York: Oxford University Press, n.d.).

## Chapter 3: Having Peace in Every Circumstance

1. For more on this, read John MacArthur Jr., *God: Coming Face to Face with His Majesty* (Wheaton, IL: Victor, 1993).

2. Thomas Watson, *A Body of Divinity* (Carlisle, PA: Banner of Truth Trust, 1986), 262.

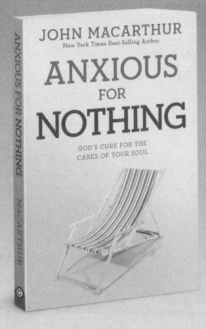

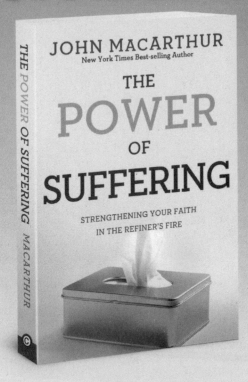

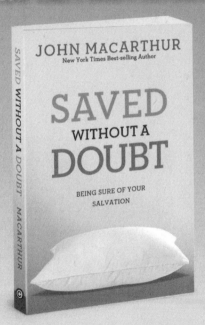